VERY
BRITISH
PROBLEMS

VERY BRITISH PROBLEMS

THE MOST AWKWARD ONE YET

ROB TEMPLE

sphere

SPHERE

First published in Great Britain in 2019 by Sphere

Copyright © Rob Temple 2019
Illustrations © Andrew Wightman 2019

3 5 7 9 10 8 6 4 2

A CIP catalogue record for this book
is available from the British Library.

ISBN 978-0-7515-7470-8

Typeset in Caslon by M Rules
Printed and bound in Great Britain by
Clays Ltd, Elcograf S.p.A.

Papers used by Sphere are from well-managed forests
and other responsible sources.

Sphere
An imprint of
Little, Brown Book Group
Carmelite House
50 Victoria Embankment
London EC4Y 0DZ

An Hachette UK Company
www.hachette.co.uk

www.littlebrown.co.uk

For everyone who suffers
from Very British Problems

CONTENTS

CONTENTS

INTRODUCTION

Hello. Unless I'm very much mistaken, you have in your mitts a beautiful copy of the new *Very British Problems* book. Look at it. Isn't it handsome? Please, rub it. Go ahead. Doesn't it feel nice? Unless of course you've obtained it on an electronic device – then it'll just look like some words on a cold, fingerprint-smeared screen. Not that I'm against technology – far from it. It's just that ... Oh dear. Can we start again?

Hello.

Well, here we go again on our own; still alive, still awkward, still ... Well, you tell me – what's it like out there? Raining? Yes, of course it is. The whole island is sodden. When we last spoke at the start of *Very British Problems Volume III*, everyone was banging on about bloody Brexit. Thank heavens that's all over, eh! And just in case that's wishful thinking and it's not yet over, I've included a whole chapter on the subject for you to stew over. Talking of stew, inside this edition there's also a section on the history of Very British Cookery (pukka!) for you to feast your eyes on/get your chops round etc. What else? I'll tell you. You'll be treated to some astrological wisdom (which I've definitely NOT just made up) as well as the greatest ever Very British Inventions, the VBP happiness scale, some spooky two-word horror stories, the top British sporting moments, a handy workplace translation guide and [pause for breath] the best places to visit within these damp shores.

If that doesn't keep you busy until Boxing Day, there's a bunch of other stuff, too – the reason being that far from dying down, the VBP epidemic is sweeping the nation like never before. VBPs are in our workplaces, in our homes, in our government buildings, in our schools, cafés, parks, rivers, cities, towns, villages, glove boxes, sock drawers ... Basically, they're inescapable. There is no vaccine. There is no cure. So there we have it, we're stuck with the malady of Britishness for the foreseeable. Nightmare, isn't it?

Ah, well. Could be worse. Not quite sure how, though, off the top of my head. Any thoughts? Answers on a postcard. I'll be in Hawaii if you need me.

Rob Temple, Cambridge, 2019

1. HAPPY NEW YEAR

Regretting making all of those resolutions
now that it's actually time to do them.

'Did you have a good Christmas?'
Translation: You better make the
most of this conversation because
it's all I've got.

'Quite quiet, really.'
Translation: I haven't the energy
to tell you.

1 January: New year, new me!
2 January: Starting tomorrow!
3 January: New year, same me!
4 January: Is the year even still new?
5 January: Worse me.

Feeling an enormous sense of achievement and well-being because you've managed to take a multivitamin for three days in a row.

Telling yourself that simply putting on your gym kit is not only 'having to start somewhere', it's actually 'half the battle'.

Giving serious thought to improving your diet, as you spread leftover pâté on your breakfast sausage roll.

Really giving your 'Good morning!' greeting some welly during your New Year's Day walk, before reverting back to an imperceptible head nod for the rest of the year.

Trying to work out which one of the 'mindfulness' apps would be the least stressful to configure.

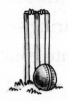

Vowing to drink only on special occasions as you crash your fifth wedding of January.

'I thought you were going for a run today?'
'I was but I had a cake instead.'

Arguing 'These contain 0% fat' while pouring sugar sachets directly into your mouth.

Wondering how the hell you're meant to slim when your cupboards still contain more chocolate than Thornton's.

Making a promise to yourself to budget only for essentials, as you add another inflatable sofa and a half-price Rubik's Cube to your Amazon basket.

Endeavouring to complete your 'From couch to 5km' goal, having successfully navigated 'From couch to kitchen' in the year just gone.

Committing yourself to a whole year of positive thinking, or at least until it all goes wrong.

Thinking your new self-help book's tip of 'Breathe' isn't going to cut it as you enter your ninety-sixth hour of filling in your tax return.

Wondering if putting a cushion on your 'bigger-than-it-looked' rowing machine will help it to better blend into your living room.

'Well, it can't get any worse.'
Translation: The apocalypse
beckons.

'This will be a great year! Touch wood!'

*Touches wood, gets splinter, screams,
disturbs large bear, gets eaten by bear.*

2. BREXIT

Featuring Brexit in a book due for release at the end of 2019 fully and sadly confident that it'll still be highly relevant.

> '**Did you vote to Leave or Remain?**'
> '**I can't even remember now.**'

Starting to panic when you realise you're now only fourth in line to be the next Brexit Secretary.

How to mime the
Brexit process in
Charades:
'One word.'
Punch
yourself
in the
face.

Filling in all your details on a 'What leaving the EU means for me' online tool, clicking 'Calculate' and getting the answer 'Dunno, pal'.

Hearing 'Oh no, not this again' and knowing someone in the house has turned on the news.

Knowing the manure has really hit the fan when someone in Parliament grabs the ceremonial mace.

Hearing someone in the Commons making a sound like a cat going through a mangle, and wondering if that means things are going well.

Preparing yourself to vote in the twelfth General Election of the year.

'The way I see it ...'
Translation: Terribly ill-informed opinion coming your way.

Going next door to ask for a cup of . . . well, everything. But no joy.

Starting to suspect that nobody involved in politics in the last three years has, at any point, had the slightest clue what's going on.

Brexit drinking game rules:
1. Take a drink every time someone mentions Brexit.
2. Get to a hospital.

Watching the news so often that you start to shout 'Order! *ORDER!*' in work meetings.

Wondering if there's any way that we could all just go back to 2012.

Trying to decide which party to vote for, now that there are twenty-eight separate ones to choose from.

You: 'At least things can't get any worse.'
The Government: 'Challenge accepted!'

'It's just a shame, really.'
'What is?'
'Britain.'

'See, that wasn't so bad!'
Translation: By some miracle we're just
about still alive. Oh wait . . .

The Year 2059: 'As a government, we promise to deliver on Brexit!'

3. YOUR VERY BRITISH ASTROLOGICAL YEAR AHEAD

We take a look at what the year ahead holds in store for you.

Aries

Thanks to your natural optimism and can-do attitude (are you even British?) a year of promise lies ahead. Travel broadens the mind but it can be expensive, so save money by staying indoors and watching *Location, Location, Location* until you feel like you've learned something new. Venus and Mars are still floating in space, as is the moon ... Keep a close eye on them.

Taurus

Don't let your natural stubbornness stop you from saying sorry. For a healthy level of Britishness, you should be apologising as many as thirty times a day. Don't hold on to toxic memories – such as that time you replied 'You too!' when someone told you to have a good birthday – let the scars heal. You're thinking about it now, aren't you? To be fair it was pretty embarrassing.

Gemini

You're a free spirit, but try not to run away from commitment this year. The new Sainsbury's may well be a lot closer and an easier drive but think of all those Clubcard points you've saved up at the big Tesco. Plus you're on first name terms with the check-out assistants now. And you really like your current Bag for Life. Do you really want to throw that all away? Saturn is in the shed.

Cancer

You'll meet someone special this year.
However, you'll walk right past them
before later thinking about all the things
you could have said. Don't let this happen!
Fall on the floor in front of them and
writhe around, guaranteeing attention.
As a water sign it's important to stay
hydrated. Before Typhoo enters the
cupboard for the first time, make a mug of
tea. Hobnobs are in ascendance.

Leo

You love to be the life and soul of the party, which is confusing for normal people who'd rather not be at the party at all, but don't let others dampen your desire to be admired. Your work ethic and focused ambition will lead you to thrive when others are binge-watching *Grand Designs* in their pants, but be wary of burn-out. Eat an antelope for energy, unless you're a vegan.

Virgo

Being the modest, humble and wise
Virgo that you are, you'll smash this year
without even realising it. Be sure to take
stock and reward yourself now and then
with a large slice of Victoria sponge. A
warning: don't let your perfectionism ruin
good relationships, unless they've fiddled
with the toaster settings again, in which
case give them hell. Pluto has been at the
gin.

Libra

You're a gentle, loving soul who finds it hard to disappoint by saying no to people. But your own needs should come first, so this year try to say no in a sneakier fashion. 'Maybe', 'we'll see', 'could do' and 'I'll see how I feel' are all very decent 'no' alternatives. If anyone sees through this plan, say 'Okay, I'll see what I can do', which, as any plumber will tell you, also means no.

Scorpio

Obsessive, possessive and jealous, if someone else has their eye on the big purple Quality Street, you'll push them into a volcano to get to it first (maybe try not to do that though). Use that intense focus for good this year. Perhaps start a project you've been putting off, or push your exercise to the next level. Or don't bother. Either, or. Mercury is cross with Venus about something.

Sagittarius

You're curious, passionate, generous and enjoy change, so you're probably not that suited to this book at all. You're just not nearly awkward enough. Try being born next month and come back. On the plus side, you're half bloody horse, which if nothing else is a fantastic conversation starter. Uranus is upset, Neptune looks sheepish.

Capricorn

Oh, practical, disciplined, cautious, stubborn, pessimistic Capricorn. You're everything Sagittarius could have been. You like to know the facts. Milk in first or last? You know it's last, and you're not afraid to say it. Perhaps, this year, try to relax and throw caution to the wind. Go out on a sunny day without a cardigan. Shout '*woohoo!*'. Jupiter has forgotten to put the bins out.

Aquarius

Being a friendly sort, you like to keep the mood light and jovial. You also like to help others, which often leaves you accidentally holding the door for wave upon wave of strangers. Indulge your inventive nature this year and create something unique, like, erm, a self-cleaning mug. Or invent Marmite-flavoured butter? Actually, no, I'm keeping that.

Pisces

Try to get more Omega 3. That's really all
the stars suggest for you. Sorry, fish face.

4. MOTORWAY SERVICES

The disappointment of taking a chance on a new motorway service station that turns out to be not a patch on your favourite.

Wondering why the parking spaces seem to be designed for cars no wider than a javelin.

Queuing fifteen minutes for a burger despite having just had breakfast and being on your way to lunch.

Being unsure as to whether £4.70 is a reasonable price to pay for a small bottle of room temperature water.

Risking flooding the forecourt with highly flammable liquid in your desperate attempts not to go over by a penny.

Paying for the top level of car wash to leave your vehicle still dirty yet covered with the maximum number of new mystery scratches.

Always managing to pick the one cubicle that appears to have been imported from day four of Glastonbury.

Noticing that the queueing system at the service-station coffee shop equates to 'Everyone mill about around the till'.

Seeing someone using the air-pressure machine and deducing they must be a highly skilled mechanic.

Pondering how many low-quality camping chairs one man needs as you squeeze another three into your car.

Trying to find a bunch of flowers that look slightly fresher than something you'd find at the bottom of your green wheelie bin.

Reading the price of petrol per litre on the big sign and still pulling in anyway because your car can't run without fuel.

Trying to remember whether your vehicle is diesel or petrol even as you squeeze the nozzle, despite owning it for over a decade.

Wondering whether to have a nice sit down on the grass/dog poo collection.

Trying to find your favourite magazine without glancing within a metre of the remarkably generous collection of adult reading.

Answering 'No' to 'Any petrol?' and worrying you don't sound nearly convincing enough.

Suspecting your life might lack excitement when you hear yourself say, 'Oh wow, they've got a Gregg's.'

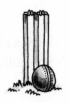

Parking as close to the entrance as possible before you get out of the car to stretch your legs.

Somehow managing to get completely lost between the car park and the motorway, in a magical place known as 'Lorry Land'.

Finally getting back on the road slightly more stressed and tired than before you stopped.

Sorted your three desk
drawers into: 'Bills and leaflets'
'Old birthday cards', and
'miscellaneous'

finding the thing you secretly
had a huge 5t over you thinking
losing, and quietly dropping in
the bin.

5. SPRING CLEANING

Sorting your three desk
drawers into 'Bills and leaflets',
'Old birthday cards' and
'Miscellaneous'.

**Finding the thing you recently
had a huge fit over your partner
losing, and quietly burying it in
the bin.**

Discovering some tinned peaches which went off in 1988, but giving them a go anyway.

Avoiding the attic as you've never been quite sure which bits you're allowed to step on.

Putting your hand in an old bag and being forced to play 'Guess what fruit I used to be'.

Wondering what 'past you' had planned when you decided to fill a box with old newspapers and then place it in the garage.

Translating 'Sort out the shed' as 'Sit in the shed for an hour and play with the tools'.

Spending half the day untangling your carrier bag full of loose wires while being certain that you did exactly the same a year ago.

'Just put it in that cupboard for now.'
Translation: Just put it in that cupboard for ever.

Visiting the charity shop and noticing they still have all your old clothes from your last clear-out.

Defrosting the freezer to discover
that you only had a single roast
potato in there anyway.

Becoming distracted for nine hours by an old mobile phone, a student cook-book and an album of holiday snaps from 2003.

Refusing to throw out an old shirt despite the possibility of you losing eight stone being dependent on time travel.

Vehemently claiming that an old bit of rotten wood discovered at the back of the garage might 'come in handy'.

'Do we really need so many condiments?' Answer: 'Yes. In fact, we need more.'

Claiming you're just nipping out to get some binbags, then driving to a lay-by to sit quietly for twenty minutes.

Changing a light bulb after a year of putting it off and being absolutely gobsmacked by how it's now not as dark.

Saying 'We really should empty that suitcase' for the fifth year in a row.

Finding the hundreds of travel adapter plugs you've purchased over the years, storing them somewhere safe and then immediately being unable to locate them.

Deciding to spend the weekend in the pub after the trauma of attempting to sort out a single bedside drawer.

6. CITY BREAKS

Time spent in city: 4 hours.
Time spent in traffic and airports: 2 days
minus 4 hours.

Wondering why you packed fifteen
different shirts yet only one pair
of trousers, which are somehow
already covered in mustard.

Saying 'According to Google Maps it's just down here', before walking a further 35,000 steps to nowhere.

Knowing it's not a proper city break unless you've angrily climbed up a 1000-step tower on a foggy day.

'Are we there yet??'
'Yes, we've literally been here for a day. This is it.'
'Oh.'

Discovering, yet again, that a famous bridge is about as exciting as most, if not all, bridges.

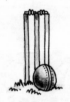

Showing that you think the hotel room is fantastic by saying 'This'll do'.

Suspecting that 'This is where they were said to have' and 'Legend has it' are both tour-guide speak for 'Nothing actually happened here'.

Asking for directions:
'*Excusee-moi*, erm, *Allez* ... the ... erm ...'
'Just over there, mate.'

Knowing that the exchange rate must really be in turmoil as you hand over €250 for a small tub of pistachio ice cream.

Wondering how long you have to stare at historical buildings before you're allowed another go in the bar.

'You should have just said if you didn't want to come.'
'I did!'

Deciding you're quite the linguist as you stroll into a bar and order two large dogs and a packet of dustbins, *danke schön.*

Accidentally getting on the wrong bus and being taken all the way back home.

Being unable to gauge the amount of euros to withdraw that lies somewhere in the sweet point between 'not quite enough' and 'a lifetime's supply'.

Taking at least one hundred photos of 'interesting' graffiti, safe in the knowledge that you'll never look at them ever again.

Saying 'It's funny how they drive on the right here' as you hurtle along in the left-hand lane.

Paying a €15 entrance fee to spend an hour honing your 'I'm actually quite enjoying this museum' impression.

Finding that the best way to explore all that a city has to offer in just 48 hours is to watch someone else do it on the telly.

Being relieved to be safely back in the sandwich section of a UK M&S.

7. THE TEN STAGES OF BRITISH HAPPINESS

How Britishly joyful are you today on a scale of 1 to 10? Find out here ...

1. 'Fine.'

Oh dear. Someone's grumpy. 'No, I'm not grumpy, I'm fine.' Yes, you are grumpy, you're in a right grump. 'I said ... I'm fine.' Really? Just that you seem a bit ... 'LOOK, HONESTLY, I'M ...' We all know what a Brit means when they say they're fine: they're not really happy, and they're only holding on to polite discourse by the skin of their gritted teeth. If a Brit says they're fine, try to stay calm and, whatever you do, don't say anything stupid such as 'chill out'. NEVER say 'chill out' to a 'fine' Brit. They'll erupt.

2. 'Been better.'

When?!

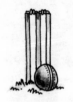

3. 'Getting there.'

Your life is falling apart. Every day is an endless trudge through thick mud to nowhere. And there's a hole in your shoe. You are quite literally getting absolutely nowhere, and you never will. It's been February for forty years, the biscuit tin is always empty and if it wasn't for tea you don't know what you'd do ... Probably sail to France or something mad. But, you know, getting there!

4. 'Mustn't grumble.'

Also known as 'Can't complain', this is
a close friend of 'Getting there', and the
two often go hand in hand. You're not
content with your situation (anything
from sore neck to tiger attack), but you
want people to know you can handle it.
It's also a coded message, meaning: 'And I
don't want to hear you complaining about
your day either.' A literal translation is
along the lines of: 'I'm fine, you're fine,
now let's talk about the weather.' But
then it also means 'Not bad' (see below).
Complicated, isn't it?

5. 'Not bad.'

You're all right, you know? You're getting by. To be honest, you haven't really thought about it in much depth. Your weekend is usually 'not bad'. Your health (if good) is often 'not bad'. It's an unthinking level of happiness. Everything just 'is'. All is plain with the world. Not to be confused with 'not too bad', which lives in an indecisive area between 1 and 10 on this chart.

6. 'Perfectly happy.'

Ah, now all is not what it seems with 'perfectly happy', else it'd be at number 10, wouldn't it? Perfectly happy means 'I'm tolerant enough of the situation, thank you, now don't push it'. 'I'm perfectly happy, thank you' is often said to a partner who's just accused you of having a face like a slapped bottom. You'll say you're perfectly happy at truly horrible events, like dinner parties, holidays, or any kind of child performance.

7. 'Yeah, not bad actually.'

You're better than expected. You almost seem a little bit surprised that you're still breathing. When people ask 'How are you?', you'll think about it a little bit, give a wry smile and realise, actually, yeeeeaah, you're not bad actually! Don't get cocky though, plenty of time left in the day.

8. 'Not too bad at all.'

Everything is just so in the 'Not bad at all' world of the Brit, but in a slightly cheeky way. It's a bit sunny. You've been to the garden centre, you're having a barbecue and a sly beer or two later. You found a new shirt you like. You discovered a fiver in an old coat. You're so happy you might even jump and click your heels together later when nobody's looking. You feel like saying 'Oi oi!' to someone. You've basically turned into Micky Flanagan.

9. 'Chuffed.'

Remember the last time you felt truly chuffed? No, me neither. Anyway, a chuffed Brit will be embarrassed about being quite this happy and won't know where to look as he or she grows ever redder in cheek. You're chuffed if you've won third prize in a local baking competition, or if you've been picked to captain your country at the World Cup.

10. 'Chuffed to bits.'

For when you've literally just found fifty million pounds, won *The Apprentice* and *Masterchef* on the same day and discovered you're immortal. Or you've just found out there's a Bank Holiday you didn't know about. There's only one level beyond this, which is 'cock-a-hoop', but no Brit has really ever reached this.

8. LOVE AND DATING

Being asked to 'say a bit about yourself' on a dating site and realising you have so few interests that you barely exist.

Proudly proclaiming that you make 'a mean crisps in a bowl'.

'I like travelling.'
Translation: I have been on holidays in my lifetime.

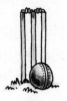

Swapping 'Would you like to go for a drink sometime?' with 'Would you like to go carpet shopping sometime?', so you can get a real view of life together.

Finding the idea of somebody requesting 'No time wasters' via the internet somewhat ironic.

Typing 'I love my job!', meaning the first thing you've said to your potential future life partner is a lie.

Interests: Tea
Hobbies: Tea
Plans: Tea
What you're looking for: Tea

Wondering if anyone on a dating app is looking for a literal 'partner in crime', and whether the police will know if you ask.

Communicating with someone completely in emojis and having no idea if it's going well.

'I'm not sure if the app's working.'
'It is working, it's just your face.'

Using a dating app when living
in the countryside, meaning you
keep getting matched with your
neighbour.

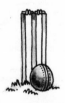

Accidentally starting a decade-
long conversation that's just you
and a stranger saying 'How's your
week going?'

The dread upon seeing that you've been matched with someone.

'How about a coffee?'
Translation: How about eight
pints and then a kebab if it goes
well?

Finding that for many people's photos,
'recent' is meant to be taken as loosely as
possible.

Thinking you've been on dating sites for too long when you start to swipe left and right on the TV remote.

Wondering if 'I really won't be too much trouble' is enough of a USP.

'We just didn't click.'
Translation: I spilled spaghetti all down
myself then fell over.

'I'm so sorry I'm late, I was sitting
in the car with my head in my
hands.'

'I don't think there was much
chemistry.'
Translation: They never showed up.

9. YOGA

Finding that people will tell you they've 'got yoga tonight' whether you asked or not.

Being told to touch your toes 'or as near as you can comfortably get', so just remaining upright.

Setting your delivery preference
for your yoga mat as 'in the loft'
just to save you a trip.

Thinking that everything you're doing is
the exception to the teacher's 'There is no
wrong way' philosophy.

'I love it, it's really good, you'd
like it.'
'Then why's your life such a
mess?'

**Really regretting your decision
to add more fibre to your diet,
after an hour of intense, nervous
concentration.**

'Yoga retreat.'
Translation: Expensive stretching
holiday.

Fearing you might have caused a scene
when your back makes a sound like a tree
branch snapping.

'Breathe if you need to.'
'But I always need to.'

Wondering why everyone's staring at you as you eat your sandwich at what you've deemed to be 'half time'.

Wishing you hadn't picked 'Horn' as your ringtone as you scrabble around in your bag while whispering 'Sorry' ten times.

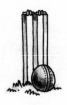

Noticing that nobody else has brought a Thermos with them.

Feeling the whole thing is one big training exercise in 'not making eye contact with anything but the ceiling'.

The awkwardness of a room full of people responding to 'How's everyone feeling?' with complete silence.

Using the five-minute relaxation period at the end to practise your 'I'm relaxing' impression.

Hoping nobody hears you opening your can of G&T.

Feeling nice and de-stressed for the two minutes it takes to get from the classroom to the traffic jam.

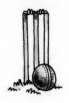

Trying to cram a twenty-minute routine into five and ending up in A&E.

Remembering the days when you and your partner did a more fun version of 'Couples Yoga'.

'I call this position: The Pint to Face.'

10. FARMER'S MARKETS

Suddenly deciding that you like
bison, having never tried it in your
life and having no idea how to
cook it.

**Wondering which one of three
exotic mustards in the rustic box
you'll throw away first.**

'It must be good – the packaging has bits
of hay in it!'

Listening to someone, for what seems like a long time, explaining exactly how they make their cheese, then saying thank you and leaving.

Hoping that someone in the family likes piccalilly seeing as you've bought a keg of it.

'Oh crikey, look how big these eggs are!'
'Did you just get excited about eggs?'
'I'm afraid so.'

Thinking you've gone over the top when you notice you're the only person dressed as a farmer, despite being in a city centre.

Realising you said, 'This venison burger isn't on par with a Big Mac' just a little bit too loudly.

'And that's the story of our chutney.'
'Fascinating.'

Realising you're walking around as if you're Prince Charles judging a vegetable competition.

Wondering how many samples of homemade vodka it's okay to try before the seller gets suspicious or you fall over.

Being just as upset as your children about the fact that there don't seem to be any rides.

'All these chocolates are homemade.'
'Not nice like Revels then?'

Trying to decide whether it's wise to buy a quiche from a pile that's been sitting in the sun all day.

Wondering whether it's worth notifying anyone that your dog just licked all the sausage rolls.

Questioning whether organic just means 'much muddier than the vegetables in Tesco'.

Trying a small bit of chilli sauce on the end of a lolly stick and immediately finding yourself unable to exhale.

'Yes, I know I said you'd be able to pet the animals – Daddy got it wrong. They've all been made into snacks.'

'Can we go home now?'
'Yes, just help me roll this pie into the boot.'

Getting home and realising the loaf of bread you purchased cost more than your last shirt.

11. NOTABLE VERY BRITISH SPORTING MOMENTS

They think it's all over! Well, it's not –
there is still loads of this book to go.
Including this bit about PE.

Sir Roger Bannister legs it

On 6 May 1954, Roger Bannister became
the first athlete to run a mile in
under four minutes (3 minutes
59.4 seconds, to be precise). He
did this while he was a junior
doctor, going on to become
a top neurologist (what have
you done today, mate?).
His record has been
unofficially beaten many
times by people running
after the 155 bus.

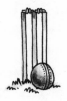

Andy Murray only goes and wins Wimbledon

This wasn't meant to ever actually happen, but it bloomin' did. In 2013, Andy Murray beat Novak Djokovic in straight sets to win the big W, despite Djokovic repeatedly hitting the ball back. Once everyone calmed down, there was a sense of . . . well, what do we do now? So Murray won it again three years later.

It just is cricket

That glorious summer of 2005, when some top-notch cricket happened (England won the Ashes) before the main event of the most raucous parade in British history. Champagne sprayed from the open deck of a bus as thousands in Trafalgar Square belted out 'Jerusalem'. Thank God Freddie wasn't driving.

Paula Radcliffe legs it for ages

Have you tried doing a marathon? Twenty-six and a bit miles? Tiring! Now imagine doing each mile in around five minutes. Without a break for lunch. This is what Paula Radcliffe had to do in 2003 to win the London Marathon with a time of 2:15:25, a record that still stands. And she wasn't even in a car!

Torvill and Dean get their skates on

It was 1984. George Orwell had predicted a bad year, but he was wrong, thanks to Jayne Torvill and Christopher Dean at the Sarajevo Winter Olympics. Dancing the 'Boléro', they became the highest-scoring figure skaters of all time. The duo now star on *Dancing on Ice*, where not everyone remains quite so upright as they did thirty-five years ago.

When football was home

Home being Wembley Stadium, London, in 1966. Then it went away, but it nearly came back home in 1990, then again in 1996, then again in 2018 ... so it should [checks watch] ... Yep, should be due back any minute, surely? It said it was only popping out for a pint of milk.

Jonny drops it ... in a good way

With 26 seconds of the 2003 Rugby World Cup Final remaining Jonny Wilkinson's drop ball connects with his weaker right foot, and for the briefest of moments time stops. Then it starts again, the ball goes through the posts and England win. Also, with the match being played in Australia, the pubs in Britain open in the early morning. Result all round.

Steve Redgrave rows to glory × 5

Row, row, row your boat, powerfully
down the stream, merrily merrily merrily
life is endless tortuous hours of
training to make you one of the
top Olympians of all time. That's
basically an ineloquent telling
of the Steve Redgrave story, the
Brit who won five consecutive
Olympic gold medals from
1984 to 2000. Legend.

Britain wins all things

Where were you on Super
Saturday? And on what day?
No, wait. Anyway, this was
that night when we won all the sport.
Jessica Ennis-Hill, Mo Farah and Greg
Rutherford took gold on the same
evening at the 2012 London Olympics.
Britain reacted by jumping up and down,
standing with hands on hips, and saying,
'I can't believe that!' over and over again.

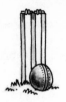

Red Rum does the treble

This thoroughbred steeplechaser won the Grand National a historic three times in the seventies and continued his fame (he even opened supermarkets) long after his racing career ended. He achieved more than you or I ever will in his thirty years on Planet Earth, and just to remind you: he was a horse.

12. FATHER'S AND MOTHER'S DAY

The horror: 'We've got the whole family coming over.'

'Don't forget to ring your dad.'
'Good point, I'll text him now.'

Insisting on being lazy all day long
'because it's Father's Day!' despite
not having children.

Wondering why your siblings always only
remind you about such occasions with
about a minute to go.

Receiving a bottle of wine that you know costs £3.99 because you buy it most days.

Wondering why you've been treated to 'hosting lots of people for a meal' as your parental treat.

Buying your dad a funny book about being a father, a topic he hasn't found funny for decades.

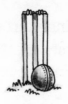

Being presented with breakfast in bed, reminding you of the time you had a lengthy stay in hospital.

Wondering if you can ask for all the sheets to be changed and washed in lieu of a substandard spag bol.

'I didn't know what to get you so ...'
Translation: I give you the gift of my company.

Presenting your dad with some sort of ornamental office supply despite him having been retired since 2005.

Struggling to find a Father's Day card when your dad doesn't like football, golf, beer or sketches of classic sports cars.

The thrill of receiving a cheaper version of the aftershave or perfume you hinted at wanting.

'You go put your feet up, I'll do the washing up!'
Eight seconds later: 'MUM ... WHERE'S THE SPONGE?'

Struggling to find a Mother's Day card when your mum doesn't like flowers, gin, princesses or glasses of prosecco.

Choosing a card that's simply
insulting to make everything a
bit less awkward.

Being amazed at how your mum and dad
manage to make their house hotter than
the average temperature of Qatar.

Finding that the whole day is a bit
like Christmas, just without the
good parts.

Being at least thankful that
Mother's Day and Father's Day
don't have songs you have to sing.

'I couldn't have asked for more
wonderful children. It's just not
something you're allowed to do.'

13. DIY

'Can I help you?'
'Do you want an answer based on past experience?'

Being told at the shop, 'We don't make those batteries any more,' rendering everything in your house inanimate.

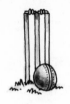

Being tempted to reply to 'We could order one in' with 'So could I'.

Getting angry at the thought of someone borrowing your socket set before you've even purchased it.

Wishing you'd written down the bulb name when it transpires there's no such one as an R2D2.

Trying desperately to resist the urge to pretend a big drill is a Tommy gun.

'Collection Point'
Translation: Empty desk with a broken bell on it.

'Well, how was I to know the saw would be sharp?!'

Deciding that you definitely require a barbecue that's larger than your car.

'Do you sell hammers?'
'What will you be using it for?'
'Ruining my house, probably.'

Having no idea why you have to mime doing some painting with the roller you've just picked up.

Walking across a warehouse behind a staff member so he can point to nothing and say, 'If we did have them, they'd be here.'

The only two amounts of paint:
1. Not enough.
2. Enough to double-coat the Taj Mahal.

Suspecting you may have revealed yourself to be 'not very handy' when you asked the difference between screws and nails.

Finding yourself testing a door handle that's attached to a wall.

'Takes two people twenty
minutes to build.'
Translation: You will never fully
build this product.

'I'm afraid we don't have them in
at the minute but you could try
another shop.'
'I know.'

Feeling like an absolute pro when you
walk into a DIY shop already covered in
paint.

'Was it a bayonet or a screw bulb?'
'Yeah, it was definitely one of them.'

Knowing that as soon as you get home you'll be on your way back.

14. PUB LUNCHING

Commenting on how they've got 'a fish board, daily specials, three salads, a tapas menu, four cuts of steak . . . ' then ordering the burger again.

'Sharing Platter'
Translation: An onion ring for you, a feast for everyone else.

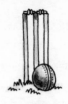

Being unable to get through the experience without someone saying: 'Do you think we order at the bar?'

Noticing the chef has forgotten to move your food from his chopping board to a dinner plate.

Getting into a lengthy debate about whether a bowl of stew with a pastry lid constitutes a pie.

The horror of receiving the text: I'm
running late, just order me anything.

Being told that if you want to order
from the full restaurant menu you
have to move one table along.

'I'm torn between the . . . choices
on all three menus.'

Hearing 'Ooh, I was going to have that', meaning you now have to sacrifice your first choice.

Realising the table you've told your child to draw on isn't actually designed for chalk.

Getting to a rural pub at 13:01 to find they've stopped serving food.

Asking for the Wi-Fi password, typing it in, noticing it hasn't worked, thanking the barman and sitting back down.

Wondering why you're paying £12 for a Scotch egg cut in half and some chips in a dirty metal bucket.

Asking 'What ales have you got?' in front of what is quite clearly the selection of ales.

'Shall we move these two tables together?'
Translation: Shall we sit at quite drastically different heights?

Asking if it's all right to have some ketchup as though you're asking for £1,000 in cash.

'But the sign says you're dog friendly?'

'Yes, but your dog ate that man's cottage pie.'

Ordering a cheese board purely for the opportunity to have another drink, even though you don't like port.

Doing the little chuckle/holding your stomach combo when saying you're too full for pudding.

Noticing the menu doesn't feel the need for pound signs, so just paying in pence.

15. TWO-WORD HORROR STORIES

Never has any list been so concise yet so chilling ...

Eye contact
Lunch meeting
Surprise party
Fancy dress

Planned engineering
Sing along
Conference call
Signal failure
Transport secretary
Role play
They're here

Rail replacement
Group hug
Team building
New voicemail
Low carb
No milk

Smart casual
Record highs
Unexpected item

Mild cheese
Wind chill
Quick word
Friend request
Your parcel
Weak flush
Going forward
Parents' evening
Tax return
Voice recording

Hen do
Expect delays
Bank balance
Happy Birthday
Fancy it?

Fun run
Improved recipe
Tequila shot
Interactive theatre
Priority boarding
Call me
Introduce yourself
Social media
Software update
Knock knock
Quite milky
Newsagent sandwich
Mini roundabout
First date
Meaningful vote

16. BUYING NEW TECHNOLOGY

Not quite knowing how to answer your partner's question 'How big is sixty-five inches then?'

Finding out the ultra-HD technology screening on the department-store display TVs will be coming to regular programming 'within the next seven to eight years'.

Wondering how many times you have to say 'great stuff' before you and the salesman can stop watching *The Incredibles* together.

Entering a phone shop knowing that 'May I help you?' actually means 'May I confuse you?'

Feeling 'Does it do Google?' was a silly question judging by the salesman's face.

Not realising that 'Plus' means 'the size of a pool table' until you open the gigantic box.

Finding life has lost all meaning at around the page 86 mark of 'big gadgets' on Amazon.

Salesperson: 'This laptop costs three thousand pounds. What are you going to use it for?' You: 'Ordering pizza.'

Accidentally changing the picture setting and spending the next year watching everything in yellow.

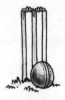

Discovering that your new headphones aren't 'wireless' – they're simply missing the required cable.

Trying to choose a phone colour that really represents your personality, so opting for light grey.

Thinking you might have gone a bit over the top with the telly size when Danny Dyer's head is larger than your sofa.

Preparing yourself to touch your new phone's screen for the very first time before noticing that you've somehow already shattered it.

Pressing 'On', being greeted with the word 'Hello!' and then spending two full days talking to Customer Support.

Updating your phone software to find your photos now only go back to 2015, which is actually a better outcome than you'd anticipated.

Entertaining your family with every single ring and text tone until you're asked to go outside.

Wondering how everyone else seems to be paying 7p a month with unlimited data when your bill costs more than your mortgage.

Being told to get something sensible and arriving home with a PC that looks like the Batmobile.

Seeing it as a bad sign that your sale purchase comes in a box that looks like it's been chewed by a lion.

Ending up with more dodgy gear on Black Friday than you'd find in Del and Rodney's van.

17. EXPERIENCE DAYS

Feeling your heart sink when opening any gift envelope that turns out not to contain cash.

Really showing your enthusiasm by asking 'When do I have to do it by?'

Really, really showing your enthusiasm by asking 'Why have you got me this?'

Driving for three hours to a racetrack so you can drive for another five minutes, then drive home again.

'Wander the grounds and soak in the views.'
Translation: Go outside.

Wishing you could swap your flying lesson for a gift that carries a little less chance of serious injury.

'Oh great, thanks, I've always
wanted to … wrestle with bears?'

Wondering if giving someone a £10 money-off voucher for Tesco counts as an experience.

'I bought you a Paintballing Experience!'
'What on earth have I ever done to you?'

Fine Dining Experience
Translation: A smaller meal than everyone else in the restaurant.

Finding that half of Experience
Days could be categorised as
'Stand in the cold for hours'.

Knowing someone really hates you when
they present you with a single ticket for a
ride on the London Eye.

Receiving an invite to a relaxing
spa day and immediately worrying
you'll arrange the towel incorrectly
at the start of the massage.

'Here are two tickets to a whisky-tasting.'
'Oh wow, thanks!'
'Do you mind driving us?'

Wondering why anyone in their right mind would feel it necessary to leave the house in order to experience wine-tasting.

Calculating whether the small sandwiches at the Afternoon Tea Experience will exceed the value of the train tickets you'll need to get there.

'Now you can learn how to make your own pasta.'
'Why?'

'We thought you might enjoy hot-air ballooning.'
Translation: We don't know you at all.

Wondering why
no company does a
Sitting Quietly And
Looking At Your
Phone Experience.

'Well, that was good.'
Translation: Well, at least that's
done now.

18. WORKPLACE TRANSLATION GUIDE

What everything said in the office *really*
means ...

'Could do.'
Nope.

'I'll have a look in a sec.'
Please go away.

'I'll sort it out tomorrow.'
I'll forget about it for ever.

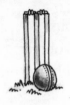

'We've had a few teething problems.'
It's been a bloody nightmare.

'What have you got on at the minute?'
Prepare for your workload to triple.

'Say that again.'
I was ignoring you but then you actually said something useful.

'Slight change of plan.'
This new, hastily-cobbled-together
plan bears absolutely no relation to
the original plan.

'She's . . . not actually here at the minute,
can I take a message?'
She's looking right at me.

'Any other questions?'
Stay silent for longer than five seconds
and we can all go home.

'Let's agree to disagree.'
You're wrong but I'm so tired.

'Lunch meeting.'
Meeting with crisps.

'I'll see what I can do.'
You're on your own.

'I'll try to make it in later.'
See you next week.

'Oh, while I'm here ...'
Everything I've said up to this
point has been filler.

'So we're all agreed?'
I'm the boss.

'I wouldn't worry if I were you.'
It's not my neck on the line. Bye!

'You're entitled to your opinion.'
You're entitled to be mistaken.

'I'm proficient in ...'
I once briefly used/saw someone use ...

'Don't quote me on that.'
What I just said was based purely
on my imagination.

'We didn't see eye to eye.'
I called him a prick, he tried to hit me,
HR got involved.

'No harm done.'
You've caused complete chaos.
Why is my desk on fire?

'It's the next thing on my list!'
I don't even have a list!

'Sorry, could you just clarify something?'
What the hell are you going on about?

'I'll admit mistakes were made.'
Total cock-up from start to finish.

'Sorry, I'm just checking an email.' I'm putting on a serious face whilst watching a video of a small dog riding a horse.

'I was literally just sending you an email.'
I was doing some online shopping until I
saw you approaching.

'That's interesting.'
I really wish you'd just shush for
a few seconds. I mean for the love
of Chri—

'I've had better days.'
This has been the worst twenty-
four hours of my life.

19. PARTY GAMES

Wishing you hadn't suggested playing a game after it leads to the break-up of your marriage.

Wondering if Truth or Dare was the most sensible game to play with your in-laws.

Shouting 'It's sodding Uranus!' as you jab your Pictionary pencil at the picture of a circle you've drawn eight times.

Getting visibly bored with Twenty Questions around the question two mark.

The horror of playing Charades with people you've only just met.

Playing a board game in a pub as an excuse to drink for a good eight hours.

Becoming so tense while watching your child play Pass the Parcel that you have to go outside and take up smoking.

Feeling like some sort of mathematical genius because you've managed to win Connect 4 a few times in a row.

Declaring, as a fully grown adult person, that you're not playing any more because it's so unfair.

Trying desperately hard not to snap at the plonker who keeps rolling the dice off the bloody table.

'Am I a bear?'
        'Yes.'
'Do I like honey?'
        'Yes.'
'Am I friends with a piglet?'
        'Yes.'
'Am I Winnie the Pooh?'
        'No.'
'YOU $£%^&*% WHAT?!'

Being furious that someone interprets the rules as they're originally written, rather than as you've always played them.

You: 'Look, shall we just call it a draw?'
Seven other people, angrily: 'NO!'

Taking your Question Card-reading duties to a John Humphrys level of seriousness.

Regretting playing Twister when you and your father have your cheeks pressed together.

Wondering if you can put 'incredibly skilled at turning an egg timer' on your CV.

Finding it hard to finish a game of Monopoly without calling it stupid and throwing the board at the cat.

Always forgetting just how violent
and spiteful a game of Musical
Chairs can become.

**Trying to work out if the game of
Trivial Pursuit will end before or
after you die of old age.**

Wondering how many different, obscure,
little-known-rules you have to make up
until you finally win.

20. GARDENING

Managing to laugh politely at your neighbour's 'You can do my hedge next!' comment, despite having painfully gritted teeth.

Going on about how much you love bees while at the same time hoping one doesn't come within twenty feet of you.

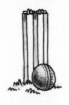

Telling someone you're going to the
garden centre, and receiving the reply
'I'll tell you where there's a good garden
centre ...'

**Being asked to just pop back to
the garden centre that's eighteen
miles away.**

Wishing you had a really neat tool shed as you lob a pair of shears in there from ten yards.

Only agreeing to go to the garden centre because there's an outside chance of a fry-up in the café.

Knowing deep down that the tomato plant you're about to buy will never produce a single edible tomato.

'Excuse me, where are the man-
eating Venus flytrap plants?'
'Sir?'
'Never mind.'

Wondering if anyone would mind if you
tested the hot tub for a whole day.

**Spending more time choosing
one of the fifty types of rake than
you did choosing your house.**

'This flowers in six to eight weeks.'
Translation: This never flowers.

Never losing the childish urge to purchase a gigantic cactus.

Being disappointed at how little 'chopping things with an axe' features in an average gardening session, but buying another axe anyway.

Wishing your partner would stop changing direction in the garden centre as your trolley has the turning circle of a 747.

Possessing gardening gloves that protect against everything except nettles, thorns and mud.

Offering to help carry compost to the car while completely forgetting that you have the strength of a child.

Discovering that 'digging a swimming pool' is as hard as everyone kept telling you.

'Do you want to come and see what I've done in the garden?'
'I've told you before to use the toilet!'

Watching your dog take five seconds to destroy the plants you just spent five hours digging into the ground.

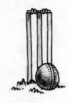

21. A HISTORY OF VERY BRITISH COOKERY

Get yourself a couple of boiled eggs and feast your eyes on this, please ...

1099

The first recorded sugar in Britain. It would take a criminal length of time before this led to the availability of Haribo Tangfastics.

1300s

The Full English Breakfast can be traced all the way back to the fourteenth century. By the 1950s half the British population started their day with it. Today, debates over what ingredients belong in a 'fry-up' can break the internet.

1390

The oldest known cookbook in the English language, *The Forme of Cury* (Forms of Cooking), contained 205 recipes written on vellum. One of these recipes: Olive Oil and Cloves. Yum!

1390s

The earliest instance of the British using mustard as a condiment is also featured in *The Forme of Cury* cookbook, marking the start of Brits thinking, 'It's not too hot actually', followed quickly by their face burning to bits.

1739

The first recipe for Yorkshire Pudding (then called 'dripping pudding') is published. From this point on, arguments would rage about whether they do or do not belong in a Christmas lunch.

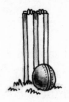

1798

London gets its first restaurant, Rules, which is still there today having survived nine changes of monarch.

1810

Sake Dean Mahomed opens the first Indian restaurant in England, the Hindoostane Coffee House, in George Street in central London.

1817

The greatest snack and sandwich filling of all time – crisps! – is featured in English optician William Kitchiner's cookbook, *The Cook's Oracle*. It would take until the 1950s before cheese and onion came into play, thanks to Irish company, Tayto.

1839

The Digestive biscuit is invented by two Scottish doctors in order to, as the name suggests, aid digestion. Many Brits argue the cure doesn't work, no matter how many packets they eat.

1902

Finally, Marmite is invented. One of the
hardest things to clean from a knife, no
matter how much you lick it, the salty
spread becomes an iconic British treat.
You either love it or you're wrong.

1951

The first supermarket is opened in
Streatham by Premier Supermarkets.
Trolley-related road rage becomes a
British hobby soon after.

1954

'Wimpy Bar' opens at the Lyons Corner House in London, becoming the first place to sell hamburger meals in the UK. The first McDonald's arrives twenty years later in sunny Woolwich.

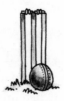

1977

Golden Wonder introduces Pot Noodle to the UK. Brits take to it with relish, partly because it's basically the food version of making a cup of tea.

1980

M&S creates the first pre-packaged sandwiches and starts a new lunch-time revolution. The first is salmon and tomato (what?), followed in 1981 by the bestseller: prawn mayonnaise.

1984

Keith Floyd slurps his way into the nation's hearts and livers with his first TV series, *Floyd on Fish*. Millions attempt to recreate his relaxed cooking style, no doubt causing an upsurge in kitchen-related accidents.

1995

Everyone's favourite aunt – Aunt Bessie – makes Yorkshire puddings a lot easier for everyone needing an emergency one in a hurry.

1999

Jamie Oliver scooters on to our CRT screens and inspires young men to whack a lot of olive oil on everything, talk like cockneys and annoy their local butcher.

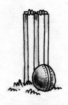

2005

John Torode and Gregg 'BIG
FLAVOURS!' Wallace introduce the
revamped *Masterchef*. Cooking would not
get 'tougher than this,' Gregg repeatedly
bellowed into our delighted chops.

2010

Get ready, get set, BAKE! *The Great
British Bake Off* first airs, a show about
strangers baking mostly not very good
cakes. In 2016, the show makes up nine of
the ten most-watched programmes of that
year.

2025

A 'roast dinner in a pill' is developed by Cambridge University scientists. Brits still ask 'Are we having mash with it?'

2032

After everyone suddenly realises how weird eggs are, the last one is eaten, in Scotch form, at a petrol station on the M6.

2038

Tea becomes edible. Other foods die out
completely. Apart from biscuits.

22. THEME PARKS

Really quite urgently needing to question whether your safety bar is properly secured, but not wanting to cause a fuss.

Getting on the dodgems and driving as sensibly as possible.

'What ride shall we go on first?'
'The car ride back home?'

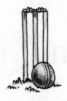

Trying to work out why a six-foot-tall
grinning rodent is making your child cry.

Wondering what culinary sorcery
theme parks pull to get food to
taste of literally nothing at all.

**Never being more panicked
and certain of death than when
coming to a halt in a water slide.**

Suspecting that
the apple in your
toffee apple has been
around longer than
you.

Looking around after an hour in
the queue and calculating that, if
anything, you've actually moved
backwards.

'Test your strength.'
Translation: Break your wrist.

Being confused as to why all theme park toilets look like the sea's just washed through them.

Discovering that the feeling of 'thrill' is much the same as the feeling of 'being annoyed'.

Spending £78 in coins attempting to win a small stuffed elephant.

Finding that 'the new ride' is always remarkably similar to all the previous rides.

Spending so long at the water park sucking in your stomach you suspect you might soon pass out from lack of oxygen.

Wondering if anyone has ever *not* been immediately sick once they've said, 'I think I'm going to be sick.'

Realising you've paid £50 to stand in a variety of differently sized queues. In the rain.

Saying 'Are you sure this is safe?' as you hurtle through the sky into the distance.

Getting home and feeding the £15 picture of you frowning on the log flume straight into the shredder.

Knowing for certain that you parked your car quite close to one of the car park's three hundred lamp-posts.

'Well, that was an experience.' Translation: Let's never do this again.

23. BONFIRE NIGHT

Thinking you can do better than the professionally organised, free fireworks display a short walk from your house.

Buying 100 sparklers for £1 and
knowing you're either going to end
up disappointed or hospitalised.

'Did you see that one?!'
'Yep, again, I managed to spot the giant
explosion.'

Fighting your sarcastic urges
when asked, 'Getting ready for
fireworks night?' as you place a
load of fireworks on the counter.

Traipsing around trying to get a
good vantage point for an event
that takes place in the sky.

**Feeling nervous when the owner
of the specialist, hard-to-find,
pop-up fireworks shop asks, 'You
sure you weren't followed?'**

Wearing enough clothes to survive a polar
expedition when attending a fireworks
display despite it being 12°C.

Feeling proud to have spent your budget on a single firework the size of a beer barrel named SUDDEN DEATH BOMB.

Trying to look like a responsible adult while placing ten rockets and three bottles of cava on the supermarket check-out.

Typing 'explosives' into Google, meaning you're now being monitored by MI5.

Being unable to say 'Ooh!' without sounding deeply cynical.

Knowing you're definitely going to buy any firework that's described as 'something a bit special' that lives 'out the back'.

Setting off an indoor firework and making your kitchen look like an explosion in a craft shop.

Asking 'Do you think it's meant to do that?' as a Catherine Wheel breaks loose and flies towards your granny's face.

Insisting on purchasing a hot dog from the stall that gives you food poisoning every November.

Wondering why you're filming it when you haven't even watched last year's video yet.

Always being puzzled as to why it takes over an hour to exit a big square field.

Wondering why everyone else in your street thinks that Fireworks Night is a month-long event.

Putting your faith in explosives from a newsagent that you wouldn't normally trust for a packet of in-date crisps.

Uttering one of three possible reviews:
'Well, that was a bit disappointing.'
'I'm sure it was better last year.'
'Is that it?'

24. THE GREATEST VERY BRITISH INVENTIONS

The Electric Kettle (1955)

The kettle: not so much an invention as a god to Brits. This humble machine provides liquid therapy at the push of a button; it offers warm hugs throughout the day. Without the kettle, tea-making wouldn't be possible (well, it would, it'd just be a right faff). For more on the history of the kettle and the making and drinking of tea, look to *Very British Problems Volume III*. In this book we're simply here to say: Thank you for your service, kettle.

The World Wide Web (1989)

At the end of the eighties, Tim Berners-Lee talked of a system that would allow researchers from around the globe to share information. The first website was launched two years later in 1991, explaining, handily, how to create websites. Fast forward to thirty years later where we mostly use the internet for arguing with strangers, watching Netflix and ordering clothes which don't fit.

The Lawnmower (1830)

Designed as an alternative to Death's favourite gardening implement – the scythe – Edwin Beard Budding, an engineer from Stroud, developed the lawnmower. He was inspired by a machine he saw in a cloth mill. Two of the earliest mowers, which featured wheel-driven rotary blades, were sold to Regent's Park Zoo and the Oxford colleges. Not one to rest on his laurels, Budding also invented the adjustable spanner in 1842.

The Fridge (1748)

You probably have a fridge in your kitchen, keeping out-of-date jars of pickle nice and cold. Well, did you know that artificial refrigeration was first unveiled at Glasgow University in the mid-eighteenth century? That's right. Scottish physician and chemist William Cullen demonstrated his discovery, the result of boiling ethyl ether in a partial vacuum. It wasn't until the next century that fridges were used for preserving food.

The Toothbrush (1780)

The first mass-produced toothbrush was created by William Addis. While in prison, he found using a rag with soot and salt less than ideal, so, using a bone from a meal and some bristles, he fashioned an alternative. By 1840, mass-produced toothbrushes were everywhere, and Addis' company, Wisdom Toothbrushes, would prosper, remaining under family ownership until 1996. It continues to manufacture tens of millions of toothbrushes a year in the UK.

The Lava Lamp (1963)

While not the most practical or brightest lamp ever, the Lava Lamp certainly provides a relaxing environment while one enjoys a few sticks of incense (and as we're on the subject, the much more businesslike Anglepoise lamp was also patented by a Brit, in 1932). British entrepreneur Edward Craven Walker, the founder of Mathmos lighting company, had the idea for the hypnotic device while watching a homemade egg timer bubbling on a stove top in a pub.

The Cash Machine (1967)

'I don't know if it's going to let me ...
WAHEY! Ten quid!' Providing the
same thrill as finding paper money in a
jeans pocket, the first cash machine to
be put into use was at the Enfield Town
branch of Barclays Bank in 1967. The PIN
technology used for security had been
patented in 1966 by Scottish inventor
James Goodfellow, who received an OBE
from the Queen in 2006.

The Text Message (1992)

Decades before the birth of emojis, 'LMAO' and WhatsApp group chats that you're stuck in until you die, the text message that started it all was sent by Neil Papworth via the Vodafone network. 'Merry Christmas', it read, which is rather nice. Much nicer was the relief Brits felt at never having to audibly speak to people ever again, lol.

Notable runners-up:

The television, the telephone, the computer, animal cloning, iris recognition, the emergency services phone number, the jet engine, the light switch, the electric clock, the pedal bicycle, the vaccine, the tin can, the telescope and The Spice Girls.

25. CHRISTMAS LUNCH

Only receiving one pig in a blanket and wondering what you've done to wrong the chef so terribly.

Considering someone to be 'not getting in the spirit of things' if they don't wear their cracker hat for at least three days.

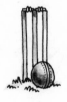

Encountering someone who thinks they're special enough to warrant the serving of a second type of meat.

'I just don't like turkey.'
'Nobody does. Eat it.'

Feeling it's absolutely essential to let everyone know where the turkey once lived.

Thinking you've done your bit by
declaring yourself 'in charge of the music'.

**Having the fascinating yearly
discussion about who does and
who does not like Brussels
sprouts.**

Noticing that whenever someone
has their 'own special way' of
doing roast potatoes, it's invariably
the same as how everyone does
them.

Asking the fortune-telling fish in your cracker why his mate didn't warn you that last year would be so bad.

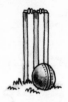

'We thought we'd have goose this year.'
Translation: We're a little bit pretentious.

'Red wine? White wine? Champagne?'
'Please.'

Saying 'Ah, this will actually come in handy!' about your cracker present, before leaving it on the table, never to see it again.

The horror: 'Remember we're spending it with my parents this year.'

Really ingratiating yourself with your host by setting off a party popper over their meal.

Trying to keep your cool as someone treats themselves to roughly a litre of gravy.

Trying to explain to Grandad that vegans probably don't want to have 'just a little bit of ham'.

Spending the meal saying 'This is really lovely, thank you' once every four seconds.

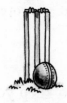

'I'm absolutely stuffed!'
'Pudding?'
'Yep. Then cheese if possible.'

Being unsure how you've managed to use ninety-two separate pans.

'What shall we do after we've washed up?'

'Sleep in a chair until the twenty-seventh.'

26. B&BS

Watching your host visibly shudder when you order six fry-ups with eight different types of egg.

'Suitable for pets.'
Translation: Covered in hair.

'We had a wonderful sleep, thank you.'
Translation: The mattress had the texture of jelly and I think my spine is damaged now.

Accidentally picking an Airbnb
that seems to involve becoming a
member of someone's family for
the duration of your stay.

Thinking you might rename your kettle
'tea and coffee-making facilities' when you
get home.

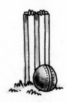

'Relax and make yourself at
home ... according to this list of
strict rules.'

Finding that the complimentary Wi-Fi takes half a day to load a web page.

Wondering when the word 'glamping' made it fun to spend £100 on sleeping in a tent in someone's field.

Being disappointed that you haven't found a single 'superhost' that actually has superpowers.

'What brings you to these parts?'
'Oh, just a wedding. I wouldn't come here by choice.'

Hoping nobody will mind that you said you won't be needing dinner, as you smuggle two clinking supermarket bags to your room.

'Here's a map of the area.'
'There's nothing on it.'
'Yes, I'm afraid it's very accurate.'

Spending a good two hours polishing your room before checking out despite the bill including a £40 cleaning fee.

Thinking you might start a B&B, before remembering how much you detest having people round.

'If there's anything I can help you with, please don't hesitate to ask.'
'Can I have a sandwich?'
'No.'

Wondering who these weirdos are that get to know the B&B owners.

Discovering that you have to order a taxi to the station at least a year in advance.

'The shower's a bit temperamental.'
Translation: You'll either get hypothermia or boiled.

Being handed a key with a key ring the
size and weight of a ship's anchor.

'What made you choose us?'
'We left it really late.'

27. DANCING

Questioning why everyone seems to think 'No, honestly, I'm fine' means 'Yes, I'd love to dance, please drag me from my seat'.

**'Why don't you like dancing?'
'Because I've seen and tried it.'**

Physically recoiling at the mere
mention of the word 'boogie'.

Finding that nothing helps your
confidence more than someone saying
'You call that dancing?'

Knowing you haven't nailed the splits when you overhear someone say 'My god, will he be all right?'

'The Twist'
Translation: One of the dances you think you can do.

Only having two sober dance moves in your repertoire: the 'I really need a wee shuffle' and 'the seizure'.

Disliking any activity where even the people who are really good at it still look absolutely ridiculous.

'The Worm'
Translation: The other one you think you can do.

Being told to loosen up a bit, so throwing in a random hand clap every now and then.

The joy of everyone forming a circle at a wedding, so you get to feel two sweaty backs for the price of one.

'Put on your dancing shoes!'
'I own hiking boots and slippers, will either of those do?'

Attempting a lift that you saw on *Strictly*, resulting in someone being put into the recovery position.

'Grease Megamix'
Translation: The wedding has
gone on too long.

Thinking you're really nailing the John
Travolta routine when in reality you look
like a drunk fighting off wasps.

Wondering just how many times
in your life you'll have to prove
to yourself that breakdancing is
actually harder than it looks.

Making sure to laugh your head off
when you go arse over tit, as if it's
all part of the fun.

**Busting out your patented end-
of-the-night move of pointing
one arm to the ceiling and
screaming along to the words.**

Being sloshed enough to convince yourself
that everyone is backing away in awe,
rather than fear.

Waking up with holes in the knees of your suit and instantly knowing you've done it again.

28. PLACES TO VISIT IN BRITAIN

Hop on the VBP open-top bus (sorry about the hail) for a guided tour of the country's wonders.

Scaffolding Ben

Previously known as Big Ben, tourists from all over the world flock to this London clock to comment that it's not as big as they thought it was.

Borough Market

Like a big Chapter 10.

Houses of Argument

A big magic building attached to
Scaffolding Ben: every time someone goes
in and out, hey presto, the country gets
worse.

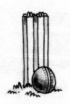

The Shard

AKA The Eye of Sauron.

The London Ferris Wheel

AKA The London Eye, AKA Old Spinny, AKA Catherine. For the full experience, visit in school summer holidays and queue for a month.

Edinburgh Castle

Home of the One o'Clock Gun, reminding the city that it's time for lunch.

The White Cliffs of Dover

The best place from which to stand and swear at the French, other than France.

Stonehenge

See the iconic prop from classic film *Spinal Tap* in all its glory.

Lack of Giant's Causeway

No giants at all. Seriously, fee-fi-fo-diddly-squat. Not even a small one. Anyway, it's in Northern Ireland, see for yourself.

Sherwood Forest

Good place to hide from the taxman.

Trafalgar Squareabout

The largest traffic island in central London boasts 56 selfie sticks per square metre as well as lions full of bored students.

Cerne Abbas Giant

A really big, rude chalk figure in Dorset.

Oxford Street

Where non-Londoners go to be stressed and say: 'This is why I couldn't live in London.'

Loch Ness

Legend has it there is no monster.

Gregg's

Created a baked good so controversial (just a vegan option) that Piers Morgan exploded.

Platform 9¾s

After a few hours of waiting in a railway station, have your photograph taken by a brick wall.

The Roman Bathtubs

Visit to see ancient bottles of Matey, some dating back to 200BC.

The M25

Britain's largest, angriest, sweariest roundabout. Accidentally drive on to it in seconds, stay for days.

Harrods

A fun way to spend an afternoon making yourself feel extra poor.

Peterborough

You can only insult a place if you're from there, so here goes ... Nah, go there, it's all right, in a way.

Wimbledon

Queue for tickets to the world's greatest tennis tournament, or for a quicker way to get in just learn tennis to a very high standard.

The London Underground

Like standing in a crowded wardrobe in complete silence, but moving.

The Post Office

Marvel as someone tries to make the process of buying some stamps last an entire lunch-hour.

The High Street

There are no shops there any more, unless you want to buy a vape, but there's usually plenty of benches for a nice sit down.

Hadrian's Wall

This one's really far up north so probably not worth it. Basically just a lot of wall. Like Platform 9¾s but older and bigger.